META

META

ODYSSEYS

CHRISTOPHER FOREST

CREATIVE EDUCATION · CREATIVE PAPERBACKS

Published by Creative Education and Creative Paperbacks
P.O. Box 227, Mankato, Minnesota 56002
Creative Education and Creative Paperbacks are imprints of
The Creative Company
www.thecreativecompany.us

Design by Blue Design
Art direction by Graham Morgan

Images by Getty Images/Allison Robbert/Bloomberg, 52, Andreas Rentz, 51, Cheng Xin, 30, Chesnot, 6, Chris Jackson, 26, George Frey/Bloomberg, 69, Juana Arias/The Washington Post, 16, Justin Sullivan, 56, Kimberly White, 64, Nicky Loh/Bloomberg, 63, OsakaWayne Studios, 12, Patrick T. Fallon/Bloomberg, 34–35, Richard Drury, 11, Rick Friedman, 20, Teera Konakan, 75; Pexels/cottonbro studio, 39, Luca Sammarco, 4–5, Pixabay, 8; Shutterstock/Shotmedia, cover; Unsplash/Adrià García Sarceda, 44, Dima Solomin, 2, dlxmedia.hu, 59, Julio Lopez, 72, Library of Congress, 24, Marie-Michèle Bouchard, 40, Mariia Shalabaieva, 60; Wikimedia Commons/Facebook, 19, Meta Platforms, Inc., 66, Olga Ernst, 70–71, TechCrunch, 48

Library of Congress Cataloging-in-Publication Data

Names: Forest, Christopher author
Title: Meta / Christopher Forest.
Description: Mankato, Minnesota : Creative Education and Creative Paperbacks, [2026] | Series: Odysseys in business | Includes bibliographical references and index. | Audience: Ages 12-15 | Audience: Grades 7-9 | Summary: "Step into Meta's evolution, from Facebook to the metaverse. High schoolers will discover how it connects global communities and shapes the future of digital interaction with bold innovation. This title includes sidebars, a glossary, selected bibliography, websites, and an index" — Provided by publisher.
Identifiers: LCCN 2025021217 (print) | LCCN 2025021218 (ebook) | ISBN 9798895811351 library binding | ISBN 9798896800880 paperback | ISBN 9798895812617 ebook
Subjects: LCSH: Facebook (Firm—Juvenile literature | Meta Platforms Inc—Juvenile literature | Online social networks—Juvenile literature | Internet industry—United States—Juvenile literature
Classification: LCC HM743.F33 F67 2026 (print) | LCC HM743.F33 (ebook) | DDC 302.32—dc23/eng/20250530
LC record available at https://lccn.loc.gov/2025021217
LC ebook record available at https://lccn.loc.gov/2025021218

Printed in the United States

CONTENTS

Facebook - Log In or Sig
://www.facebook.com
To help personalize content, tailor and measure ads, and provide a safer experience, we use cookies. By clicking or navigating the site, you agree to allow our collection
information on and off Facebook through cookies. Learn more, including about available controls: Cookies Policy.
facebook
Email or Phone
Password
Need help?
Sign Up
It's free and always will be.
Connect with friends and the world around you on Facebook.
See photos and updates from friends in News Feed.
Share what's new in your life on your Timeline.
Find more of what you're looking for with Facebook Search.
First name
Mobile number or email
Re-enter mobile number or emai
New password
Birthday
Month
Day
Year
Female
Male
By clicking Sign Up, you agree to our Terms and
read our Data Policy, including our Cookie Use
Sign Up
SAMSUNG

Introduction

An adult arrives home after a long day of work. She kicks back on the couch and glances at her cellphone. She has received a Facebook notification.

She signs into her Facebook account and gets a message from a friend she hasn't seen since middle school. As she replies to her friend, she sees a "friend request," from another friend that she went to college with.

OPPOSITE: The creation of Facebook set the stage for all other social media platforms.

After that, she scrolls through posts made by several acquaintances. She ends her session by looking at a posting of upcoming events in her town and finds two she is interested in attending. She clicks on the "interested" button and then signs off. Meanwhile, her thirteen-year-old son is sitting at the other end of the couch. He is on his cellphone checking his Instagram account. He is reading a post from his favorite basketball player. Then, he checks out the latest Instagram reel from his favorite musician.

Millions of people take part in these rituals every day. It has helped make Facebook, Instagram, and its parent company Meta, a social media powerhouse. In fact, as of 2021, nearly three billion people have signed up to use Facebook.

In The Beginning

On February 4, 2004, students at Harvard University in Massachusetts were presented with a unique opportunity. They were invited to join a new social media site called "The Facebook." Sophomores Mark Zuckerberg, Eduardo Saverin, Chris Hughes, and Dustin Moskovitz worked hard to produce this site. They intended to have a place where students on campus could connect and **network** with other students.

OPPOSITE: While the website started at Harvard, Mark Zuckerberg dropped out following Facebook's success.

They borrowed the idea from the "Face Books" established by Harvard University. These "Face Books" were directories showing each student's name and photo, helping Harvard students get to know each other. Students could create personal pages where they could share photos, list club affiliations, and even outline upcoming events and their daily schedules.

The site's success led to its expansion, and by the summer of 2004, students from 34 colleges—including institutions like Stanford and Yale—had joined. More than 250,000 students had established profiles on the site.

The rapid popularity of the site also attracted business interest. For example, the credit card company MasterCard approached the founders about advertising opportunities. This allowed the site to make money. Before long, Facebook became a phenomenon.

Zuckerberg and his classmates knew they were onto something big. By the end of 2004, Facebook had introduced features such as the 'Wall'—a space where users could post messages, share birthday wishes, or congratulate friends on a new job.

The new features brought even more users to Facebook. More than one million students had created profiles by that time. The site was beginning to rival the popular site MySpace, which had over 5 million users at the time.

9.0 Optimized SE provided by Dell®
Edit
Mail
Community
Services
Safety
Window
Keyword
Write
IM
People
Safety
Settings
Music
Finance
http://gwu.thefacebook.com/profile.php?
Sarah (Svetlana) Schafer's Profile
quick search
go
Picture
[edit]
Information
Account Info:
Name:
Member Since:
Last Update:
Basic Info:
Contact Email:
School Email:
Status:
Sex:
Year:
Concentration:
Residence:
Birthday:
Home Town:
High School:
Extended Info:
Screenname:
Cell:
Looking For:
Interested In:
Visualize My Friends
Edit My Profile
America Online 9.0 O...
WordPerfect 11 - [Do...

OPPOSITE An early Facebook profile

In 2005, Facebook made three important changes. First, they allowed users to post unlimited photos. This means they could add as many pictures as they wanted. They introduced a **tagging** feature that allowed users to identify friends in their photos, automatically notifying those tagged. If the person had a Facebook account, they would get a notification saying a photo with them in it had been added. This eventually became one of the most popular features on Facebook.

However, the biggest change from that year involved access to the site. The owners began to allow college students outside the United States to join. They even opened access to students in high school. Students across the globe were posting on each other's walls, adding pictures, and tagging friends worldwide. This allowed

Facebook to reach users across the globe. As 2005 came to an end, Facebook had grown to six million users.

Facebook's popularity convinced the owners to take a bold, new initiative. They decided to open Facebook to anyone over the age of 13. Zuckerberg and others believed this would further enhance the profitability of Facebook. It did. Advertisers took notice. They created pages and advertising campaigns aimed at Facebook users.

As Facebook grew bigger, the company continued to roll out new features. However, not all proved popular. In fact, Facebook ran into its first problem with users in 2006. That year they unveiled a feature called News Feed. The News Feed feature allowed a user to be notified about each change a friend made to their Facebook page. News Feeds were flooded with changes. This annoyed some users because they would get a daily list

Initially launched in 2009, the “like” button provided a simple way for users to express approval without leaving a comment.

Techie at an Early Age

Mark Zuckerberg's name is often linked with computer coding—and for good reason. He started coding before his teen years. By age 12, he used the BASIC language to build online applications, including "Zucknet," a messaging system his father used in his dental office. It let computers in their house and the office communicate, allowing his father to talk to his receptionist from home. A few years later, Mark built a media player that could "learn" users' music preferences.

of changes. Other users felt that the News Feed was an invasion of privacy.

Facebook continued to challenge other social media competitors as it grew. It surpassed My Space in popularity by 2008, and became the most visited social media website.

The company also faced off against Twitter, a social media site now known as X. Twitter includes a feed where users could post short clips of news, stories, or facts about their own lives. Facebook adopted a similar feature called Live feed, where facebook users posted their own news, stories, or facts. It would be shared on the homepages of other friends, to keep them up to date with recent posts. The feature became popular. It still exists today but has been merged with the News Feed.

When the 2008 presidential race rolled around, Facebook had established itself as a social media force. However, the company was soon about to tackle politics. That happened with the 2008 presidential race between

Democratic candidate Barack Obama and Republican candidate John McCain.

Without intending it, Facebook became the internet face of the election. Savvy **political advisors** realized the potential to use Facebook to share the points of view of each candidate. Multiple pages were created to support each candidate.

Barack Obama made his presence known on Facebook early. He was able to use it to help him outmaneuver Hillary Clinton. Obama ran against her in the Democratic **primary election**. He tailored his main Facebook page during the presidential election to appeal to a broader audience. He listed favorite musicians such as Bob Dylan and Stevie Wonder, as well as Miles Davis. He noted that he liked to play basketball and enjoyed "loafing w/

Obama was able to captivate voters partially through his online presence

kids" as pastimes. Meanwhile, John McCain had his own main page. He listed a favorite pastime as fishing and listed Letters from Iwo Jima as his favorite movie.

More than 1000 pages were created to support the candidates. When Facebook users compared the two candidates, they often found Obama's **online presence** more appealing. Barack Obama won the election in 2008. Experts declared that the "Facebook effect," or his presence on Facebook helped him win. In the end, that should have come as no surprise. During his campaign, Obama relied on Chris Hughes, one of the original Facebook founders, for advice. This proved helpful in securing Facebook fame.

Since that time, Facebook has been at the site of many other political movements throughout the world.

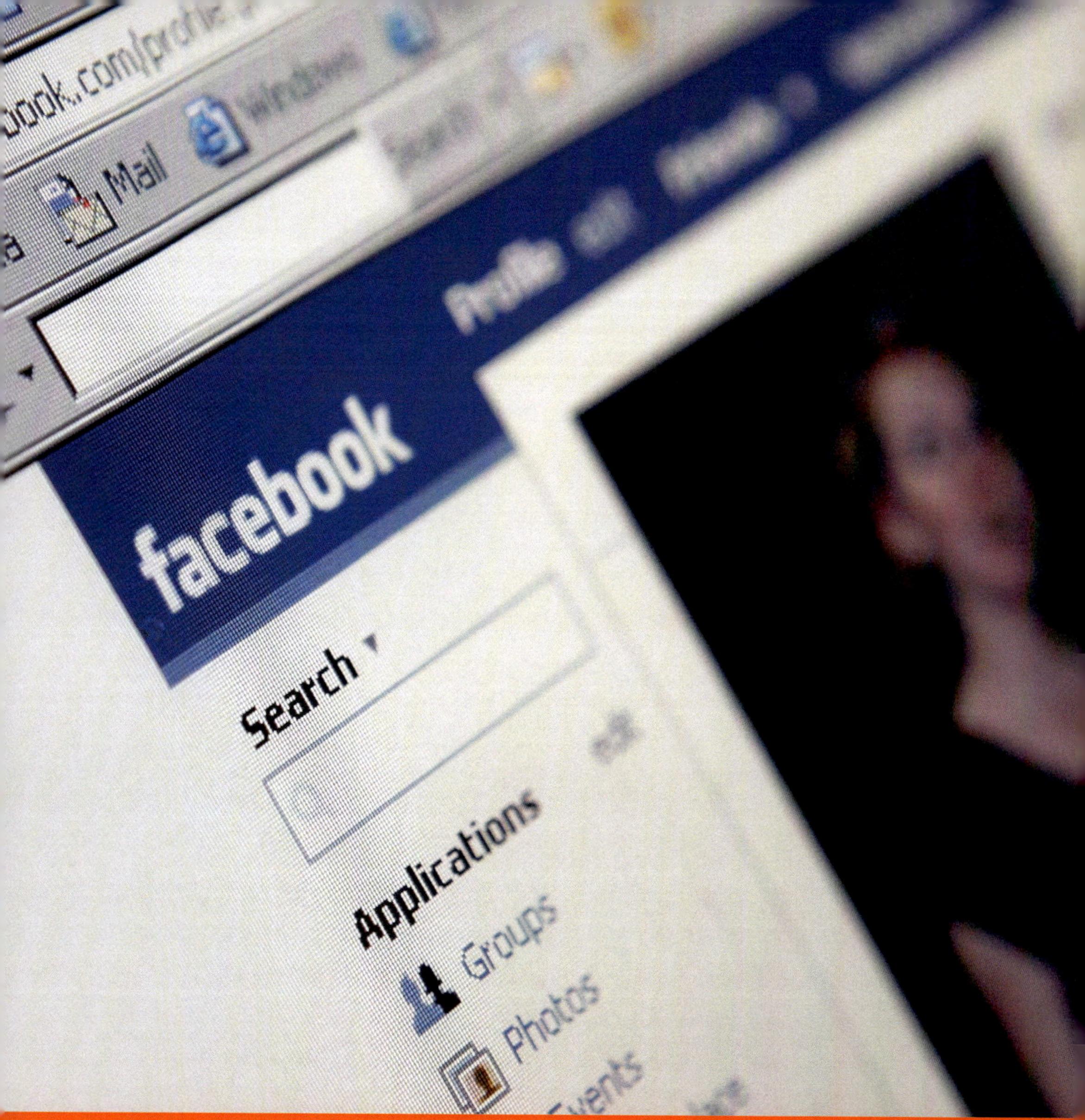

First Attempt at Facebook

Before creating The Facebook, Mark Zuckerberg launched two other websites at Harvard. The first, CourseMatch, helped students see which classes their friends were taking. The second, Facemash, let users rank students' attractiveness using photos pulled from Harvard websites—without permission. It attracted over 22,000 views in a day but was quickly shut down by Harvard, and Zuckerberg was forced to apologize or face expulsion.

In 2012, Facebook took its next giant step. It decided to "go public." This meant that it decided to sell shares of **stock** in the company to the public. A stock is a small part of a company that another person owns. The money Facebook raised by selling stock would be used by the Facebook to invest in its own company. It could improve technology, expand its operations, and make upgrades to the platform.

Going public proved successful. Facebook was able to raise 16 billion dollars by the end of the initial offering. At the time, this was the largest ever offered for internet stocks. Allowing the public to buy stock also changed the ownership structure of Facebook. Because people could buy stock in the company, they owned small individual shares. However, Mark Zuckerberg held 13 percent of the stock—more than any other owner. This made him a **majority owner**, with control over the company.

On October 28, 2021, Zuckerberg announced that Facebook would be undergoing a name change of sorts. From then on, the parent company that owned Facebook would be known as Meta. The name comes from the Greek word for "beyond." However, Zuckerberg hoped the name would also mean something else to users.

"Over time, I hope that we are seen as a metaverse company. I want to anchor our work and our identity on what we're building toward," Zuckerberg stated during an online meeting.

Along with the name change came a new logo. The blue infinity symbol became Meta's official logo, symbolizing the possibilities of the metaverse.

The metaverse itself is a place that doesn't exist now. Zuckerberg aimed to help build an online digital world where people could collectively work and exist online. They could share stories, communicate, and even play games in a digital utopia.

Koum had a brainstorm about creating a new type of **application** that would allow people to communicate about their work status while on the job.

16:38
WhatsApp
WhatsApp Messenger
Simple. Reliable. Private.
Open
15M RATINGS
4.7
AGE
12+
Years Old
CHART
#2
What's New >
Version 24.22.3
Preview
Simple.
Reliable.
Private.

Meta Expands

Most people associate Meta with Facebook, but Meta also owns other social media companies beyond Facebook. Another notable platform owned by Meta is WhatsApp. WhatsApp was created by Jan Koum and Brian Acton in 2009. The two friends met while working at Yahoo, an internet company, and left in 2007.

OPPOSITE: Whatsapp has become one of the most popular messaging apps ever created, with users across the globe.

Koum originally designed the app for iPhones, and Acton soon joined him in running the company.

The two friends soon realized they had a bigger application and developed an Android version. This update allowed users to send messages between different devices. For example, a person could send a message from an Apple iPhone to an Android device without losing part of the message. At the time, this was not easy to do between the two platforms. They eventually began

> "IN 2014, FACEBOOK ACQUIRED THE APP FOR $19 BILLION."

charging users for the service, and by 2013, the app had reached 200 million users.

In 2014, Facebook acquired the app for $19 billion, eventually making it free for users two years later. Facebook began sharing data between WhatsApp and itself to target ads to users. However, this policy proved problematic for many users. Many users complained that this new policy was a violation of their privacy. Critics felt that WhatsApp did not protect privacy enough. As a result, Facebook worked to improve the security and privacy of the users.

Founders of WhatsApp, Acton (L) and Koum (R)

These challenges led to the departure of the original founders, Acton and Koum, by 2018. WhatsApp continued growing and expanded to 180 countries, eventually gaining more than 2.2 billion users. Yet, the application still has received criticism over the years. Some people view it as a haven for **extremists** to share their opinions with other people. Others believe it has helped lead to the spread of disinformation throughout the world. Some countries, such as China and Iran, have entirely banned the service.

Another social media platform owned by Meta is Instagram. Facebook acquired the popular application in 2012.

Instagram launched in 2010. It was initially created by Kevin Systrom, who attended Stanford University and spent time working for Google. Systrom was inspired by other social media platforms that allowed users to quickly share their locations along with pictures. He called his service Burbn.

Systrom sought help from fellow Stanford graduate Mike Krieger, who offered technical experience. The two of them worked hard on the Burbn application and made two important changes. First, they decided to focus on creating an application where a person could take a picture with their mobile phone. They could then post the picture, along with a short message, "instantly" to the site. This led them to rename their application, Instagram.

They continued refining the app to take full advantage of the new iPhone's enhanced camera capabilities. They thought it would be a hit. They began testing the application by posting photos on the improved platform in July, 2010. On October 6, 2010, they released Instagram on Apple's App Store. The app drew 25,000 users on its first day and hit one million within three months.

Instagram's popularity exploded. Within months, other companies were contacting the founders, trying to purchase the application. Facebook finally made a deal to purchase the company for $1 billion in cash and Facebook stock in April 2012.

Under Facebook's ownership, Instagram continued to grow, adding features that allowed users to post pictures,

A Good Move

When Facebook bought Instagram, the app had just 13 employees and had recently launched its Android version. Mark Zuckerberg assured users it would stay independent, letting people share photos across various platforms—not just Facebook. The move paid off: by early 2013, Instagram had surpassed 100 million users.

send private messages, upload videos (now known as reels), and share stories that disappear after 24 hours As of April 2024, Instagram, had more than 2 billion users. It is the third most popular social media platform behind Facebook (number one) and Youtube (number two).

In 2014, Facebook ventured into the **virtual reality** market by acquiring Oculus for $2 billion.

Oculus got its start two years earlier. It was the brainchild of Palmer Luckey. Luckey fell in love with the idea of virtual reality at an early age. He began collecting virtual reality headsets when he was a teen. However, he grew frustrated with the poor performance, believing they didn't function as well as they should. In his spare time, he began building his own headsets using spare parts from the models he collected. Meanwhile, he attended California State University, Long Beach part-time to study journalism while also working at USC's mixed-reality lab.

Luckey did not start off planning to build a technology company. He just wanted to develop a better headset for his own use. Then, perhaps, he could interest other people in buying them. It might be a **side hustle**. However, Luckey had a stroke of good fortune. He encountered a software programmer and business owner named John Carmack. Carmack had helped create popular games such as Wolfenstein 3D and Doom.

> "WITHIN ROUGHLY TWO YEARS OF ITS FOUNDING, OCULUS WAS ACQUIRED BY FACEBOOK."

During their conversation, Carmack mentioned that he had been planning to rebuild a pair of VR goggles to improve their performance, prompting Luckey to explain that he was already developing his own version. Carmack became intrigued. He saw one of Luckey's headsets and asked if he could buy it. Luckey was such a fan of Carmack's work that he gave him a headset for free.

Luckey had no idea his breakthrough was about to change everything. Carmack demonstrated the headset at a convention. Almost instantly, word spread that Car-

Virtual Skill Building

Oculus headsets have influenced fields far beyond gaming, becoming valuable tools in therapy, education, and professional training. In mental health, Virtual Reality Exposure Therapy (VRET) helps people face phobias, PTSD, and anxiety in a controlled, immersive setting, while calming VR environments support stress relief. In medicine, VR lets surgeons and students practice procedures through risk-free simulations, boosting precision and confidence. Education benefits from interactive lessons that let students explore subjects like history, science, and engineering in dynamic virtual spaces. Corporations and emergency services also use VR to simulate high-risk situations, helping employees build critical skills safely and effectively.

mack was embarking on a new VR project. The headset caught the attention of other technology giants. Soon, Luckey raised money to launch his own company, Oculus.

In less than two years, Oculus had raised millions of dollars and developed several headset models. Carmack even left his job at the company he cofounded to join Luckey's company. The popularity of the product caught the attention of Facebook. Within roughly two years of its founding, Oculus was acquired by Facebook. Soon, it joined the Facebook family of companies.

Over the years, the company has undergone several **rebrandings** and is currently known as Meta Quest.

Meta Controversies

Although Meta long been a dynamic social media **conglomerate**, it has also been involved in a variety of controversies. In fact, the first controversy began shortly after the site was launched.

In 2007, twin brothers Cameron and Tyler Winklevoss, along with Divya Narendra, took Mark Zuckerberg to court. The former Harvard students contended that Zuckerberg stole the idea for Facebook from them.

According to the trio, they first met with Zuckerberg when they were all students at Harvard, with their initial meeting taking place in October 2003. By that time, Zuckerberg had already gained a reputation as a skilled coder on campus. The three approached him for assistance in developing a social networking site they called Harvard Connection.

Harvard Connection was intended to help students connect online by using their Harvard email addresses to build both social and professional networks. Because they planned to restrict the site to Harvard students, they believed it would be safe and secure.

Over the next three months, the trio met with Zuckerberg several times to discuss the website's design, exchanging more than 50 email conversations about its development. However, the Winklevoss twins and Nar-

OPPOSITE The Winklevoss Twins in 2015. Their dispute with Maerk Zuckerberg is one of META's earliest controversies.

endra were unaware that Zuckerberg had already begun tinkering with his own social media website.

A few days before their fourth meeting, Zuckerberg registered the domain name "thefacebook.com." When Zuckerberg launched The Facebook in 2004, the Winklevoss twins and Narendra learned about it through *The Harvard Crimson*. They were stunned by how closely it resembled their Harvard Connection concept.

The trio's relationship with Zuckerberg deteriorated. Although they eventually launched their own site—later renamed ConnectU—they felt betrayed as Zuckerberg's site skyrocketed in popularity. This perceived betrayal led them to file a lawsuit.

After many tense meetings and negotiations, Zuckerberg maintained that he had developed Facebook independently, arguing that the concept of a social networking site was hardly original—especially since other platforms, such as MySpace, had existed before either The Facebook or ConnectU. Despite these arguments, the Winklevoss twins and Narendra persisted in their legal battle.

In 2008, an arbitration process culminated in a settlement in which Facebook paid the trio a total of $65 million. They later sought additional compensation in an appeals court, but a three-judge panel upheld the original award.

Privacy concerns have long plagued Meta and its flagship product, Facebook. The first hints of concern followed the development of the News Feed feature. While the feature was later adapted and the controversy calmed down, new privacy issues have arisen over the years.

Facebook Goes Hollywood

In 2010, Facebook's story hit the big screen with The Social Network, based on Ben Mezrich's book Accidental Billionaires. The film offered a fictionalized account of Facebook's founding and the surrounding drama. Though popular, it drew criticism for taking artistic liberties with the founders' stories and controversies. Some viewers also disliked the portrayal of Zuckerberg as "humorless" and "heartless." The movie implied he created Facebook to meet women, rather than to help college students stay connected.

Zuckerberg departs federal court

One significant problem arose in 2007 with the launch of Beacon—a Facebook program that allowed companies to track users' purchases and notify their Facebook friends about those transactions, often without the users' consent. This practice sparked considerable backlash, as many users did not want their purchase histories publicly shared. Zuckerberg eventually apologized for Beacon and the unintended consequences of the program.

Privacy issues were also at the center of a legal battle between Facebook and the **Federal Trade Commission** (FTC) in 2011. The focus of the problem between the company and the FTC was the amount of user data that third party applications and advertisers could access. Facebook contended that the applications and advertisers could only access data they needed to operate on Facebook.

However, after further investigation, it became clear that Facebook misrepresented the amount of data that applications and advertisers could access. It turned out that almost all user data was accessible. This was viewed by the FTC – and users – as a major privacy violation. As a result, in 2011 Facebook had to agree to undergo an independently run evaluation of their privacy policies every other year for twenty years.

Meta has faced several controversies over the spread of fake news, with the most notable involving misinformation during presidential elections. The first dramatic occurrence of this happened during the 2016 presidential election between democratic candidate Hilary Clinton and Republican candidate (and eventual winner), Donald Trump.

During that election, users posted misleading and false information about the election and its candidates. In 2016, international operatives—particularly from Russia—exploited Facebook by repeatedly disseminating inaccurate information, often targeting Hillary Clinton in an effort to sway the race. Similarly, during the 2020 election, Facebook became a hotbed for misinformation

A Name Change?

Facebook's 2021 rebrand to Meta puzzled some, as its name was already recognized by billions. While the company stated the change reflected its vision for the metaverse, many marketing experts saw deeper motives. By then, Facebook had faced mounting controversies, and companies have historically rebranded to shift public perception. Some argue that Meta is more about reputation management than futuristic innovation.

concerning COVID-19, voter fraud, and mask mandates, all aimed at influencing voter behavior.

Facebook addressed the problem through multiple measures. First, the company changed the **algorithms** used in coding. This began to push political information further down on its list of new traffic. People were far less likely to see political posts show up in the feeds by the 2024 election. Facebook also hired more people to track security and safety issues worldwide. This helped prevent misinformation and illegal access to the site. Along with this, Facebook even developed a fact-checking service that included a partnership with other news agencies and independent fact-checkers. This allowed agencies and fact-checkers to fact-check posts on Facebook and report when misinformation was being spread.

“META DECIDED TO REPLACE THE ACTUAL FACT-CHECKING SERVICE WITH A COMMUNITY-BASED SYSTEM ON ALL OF ITS PLATFORMS.”

Although the service was helpful, problems with misinformation continued to spread during the 2024 election. As a result, the fact checking service ended in January 2025, causing its own controversy. Meta decided to replace the actual fact-checking service with a community-based system on all of its platforms. This allowed users to monitor content. They could report misinformation and direct others to more ac-

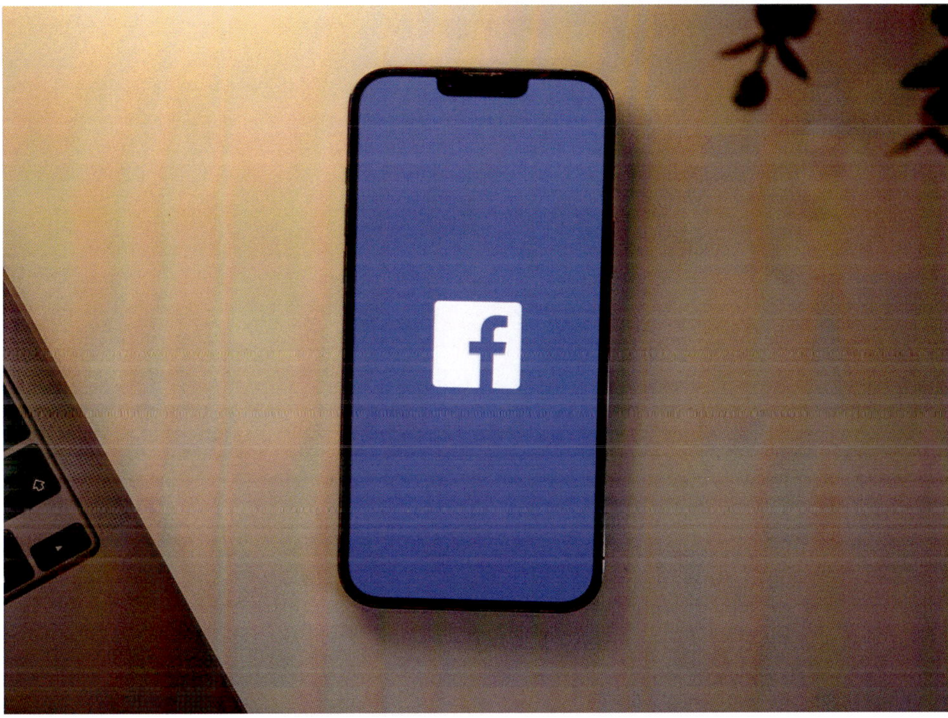

curate, complete information. Although not all users believe that this new system will be effective, Meta argues that it is a better method for combating fake news while continuing to allow its security teams to monitor dangerous content.

Meta Evolution

Facebook has transformed dramatically over the years, going far beyond a simple name change. It hardly resembles the company that was started in Mark Zuckerberg's college dorm room. While Zuckerberg remains with the company, Saverin, Hughes, and Moskovitz are no longer part of it.

OPPOSITE: The meta logo has changed significantly over the years, as the company moves away from it's Facebook origins.

OPPOSITE Eduardo Saverin

Eduardo Saverin was the first to leave the company he helped launch. He became involved with Zuckerberg when he was a junior at Harvard and invested around $19,000 in the startup. Serving as the initial financial officer and business manager, Saverin remained with Facebook until 2005. Accounts suggest he departed following a disagreement with Zuckerberg over the value of his shares—when it appeared that Zuckerberg was attempting to consolidate power, Saverin left and subsequently began investing in other companies in Asia.

Chris Hughes was among the original team members and one of the early investors in Facebook. Notably, of the core founders, he was the only one without a background in technology—having gone to Harvard to study history and literature. Hughes contributed by working on the site's **user-friendliness** and functionality. He remained

Friends to Enemies?

Although they co-founded Facebook, tensions grew between Eduardo Saverin and Zuckerberg as Zuckerberg sought outside investors and moved the company to Silicon Valley while Saverin stayed in New York. Their conflict peaked when Zuckerberg diluted Saverin's shares from 30% to under 10%, effectively removing him. Saverin sued for unfair treatment, settling in 2009 with a financial payout and a small stock percentage. Despite the legal battle, Saverin remains a billionaire from his early stake, though he and Zuckerberg no longer work together.

Dustin Moskovitz

with Facebook until 2007, when he left to join Barack Obama's presidential campaign, where he managed the future president's online presence. Hughes continued to hold facebook stock for some time after his departure.

Dustin Moskovitz was Zuckerberg's dorm roommate at Harvard and is widely recognized as one of Facebook's co-founders. He was present during the early days (and even during the creation of projects such as Facemash) and helped write code for Facebook, earning a reputation as one of its first "marathon coders." He also

Meta AI logo

served in an early leadership role in technology (often described as the company's first chief technology officer). Moskovitz remained with Facebook until 2008, when he left to cofound Asana with another former Facebook employee. Asana is a company that develops tools to help organizations manage work and projects online.

“ONE AREA THAT META PLEDGES TO FOCUS ON IS ARTIFICIAL INTELLIGENCE (AI)”

Meta's evolution has been a constant throughout its history. As it has grown and added new platforms to its portfolio, Meta has emerged as one of the dominant forces in social media. Change will continue to be integral to Meta's identity even as Facebook enters its third decade.

One area that Meta pledges to focus on is **artificial intelligence (AI)**. The company is investing heavily in AI initiatives, hoping to integrate these technologies into future products and services. For example, AI now plays a central role in determining whether content posted on Facebook is appropriate or inappropriate, and it drives the content that users see in their feeds.

Meta also plans to rely more on renewable sources of energy. The company has established a "net zero" plan that includes incorporating additional solar and wind energy to power its operations. This initiative is expected to help reduce Meta's **carbon footprint** and move the company toward 100 percent sustainability.

Furthermore, Meta's popularity should continue to grow worldwide. Mark Zuckerberg has pledged to

Mark Zuckerberg in 2020

Saving the World's Water

Meta has developed ways to be sustainable and reduce its carbon footprint. But did you know that Meta is also working to save the world's water supply. Starting in 2017, Meta began working in areas where its office buildings are located to undertake water restoration projects. These are efforts to improve the watersheds in such regions. These efforts include improving access to water, improving water sanitation and hygiene, and restoring ecosystems. Currently, Meta is working on projects in six states, including California, Arizona, and Texas.

Meta

OPPOSITE Threads is a text-based social media platform launched by Meta in July 2023 as a competitor to Twitter.

bring Internet access to the entire world within the next decade—a commitment that, if fulfilled, could drive significant user growth. For instance, one forecast predicts that by 2028, the number of Facebook users in the United States will reach a new high of 262.8 million.

As Meta expands and pursues "greener" practices, it continues to generate a steady **revenue** stream from advertisers. This reliable revenue should help sustain the company through the 2020s. Analysts predict that, along with savings from green initiatives,

Meta's financial performance will benefit its stockholders. For example, while Meta stock closed 2024 at around $585 per share, some Wall Street experts forecast that it could reach $995 per share by 2030.

Clearly, Meta's evolution demonstrates how platforms can adapt as times change—a goal that appears to be integral to Meta's strategy as it moves closer to realizing its vision of a true metaverse.

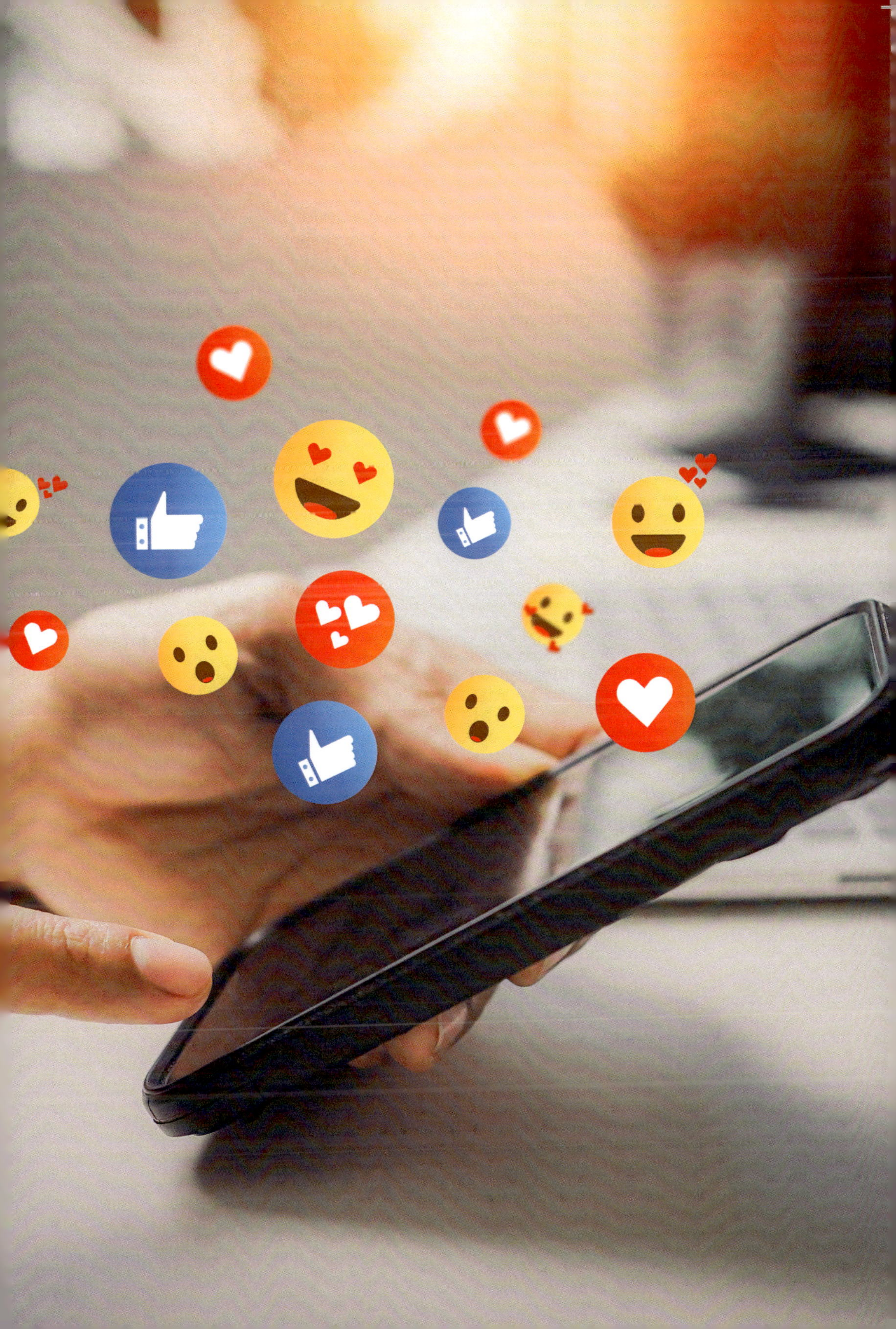

Selected Bibliography

Antonio, Jose. "The Face of Facebook." *The New Yorker,* 13 Sept. 2010, www.newyorker.com/magazine/2010/09/20/the-face-of-facebook.

Biography. "Mark Zuckerberg - Facebook, Family & Facts." Biography, 24 Oct. 2019, www.biography.com/business-leaders/mark-zuckerberg.

Hall, Mark. "Facebook." Www.britannica.com, 30 Mar. 2024, www.britannica.com/money/Facebook.

Kaplan, Katharine A. "Facemash Creator Survives Ad Board | News | the Harvard Crimson." Www.thecrimson.com, 19 Nov. 2003, www.thecrimson.com/article/2003/11/19/facemash-creator-survives-ad-board-the/.

Mezrich, Ben. "How Mark Zuckerberg Battled the Winklevoss Twins over a $65 Million Facebook Settlement." *Vanity Fair*, 30 Apr. 2019, www.vanityfair.com/news/2019/04/inside-the-mark-zuckerberg-winklevoss-twins-cage-match?srsltid=AfmBOoqRI-QD1A9hOJru2MpXU1SMFwzFZwBUcneG6VRVFxmWkTuY_akK. Accessed 20 Jan. 2025.

NDTV News Desk. "Programming Prodigy to Meta CEO: Inside the Life of Mark Zuckerberg." Www.ndtv.com, NDTV, 22 Oct. 2024, www.ndtv.com/people/programming-prodigy-to-meta-ceo-inside-the-life-of-mark-zuckerberg-6848033. Accessed 20 Jan. 2025.

Soumitra Dutta, and Matthew Fraser. "Barack Obama and the Facebook Election." US News & World Report, *U.S. News & World Report,* 2019, www.usnews.com/opinion/articles/2008/11/19/barack-obama-and-the-facebook-election.

Travers, Mark. "Facebook Spreads Fake News Faster than Any Other Social Website, according to New Research." *Forbes,* 21 Mar. 2020, www.forbes.com/sites/traversmark/2020/03/21/facebook-spreads-fake-news-faster-than-any-other-social-website-according-to-new-research/

Glossary

Algorithms a set of instructions to determine what content is shown on a social media platform

Application a program written to complete a task or purpose

Artificial Intelligence the development of computer technology to perform tasks usually require humans to perform

Carbon footprint the amount of greenhouse gases that are produced by a person, object, or industry

Conglomerate several different businesses that are part of one business

Extremists people who hold fanatical political positions

Federal Trade Commission an American governmental agency that enforces laws to protect consumers

Majority owner a person or company that controls enough shares of a company to control voting power

Network to connect with people with similar jobs, education, or beliefs

Online presence the way a person, company, or brand name is represented online

Political advisors people who aid, support, and advice to politicians

Primary election an election to choose a candidate to run in a final election for office, such as a candidate running for president for a major political party

Rebrand an effort to change the image of a company

Revenue the total amount of money a company makes

Side hustle a way a person makes money in addition to the main job they have

Stock a publicly traded share of ownership of a company

Tagging attaching the name of a person to a picture on social media

Virtual reality an environment created by a computer the simulates reality

User-friendliness the quality of how easy a product is to access, use, and understand

Websites

Meta

https://www.britannica.com/money/Meta-Platforms
Read facts about the Meta company

A Brief History of Meta and The Evolution of Facebook

https://www.big3.sg/blog/a-brief-history-of-meta-and-the-evolution-of-facebook
This site explores the background and history of the Meta company

Beginners Guide to Instagram

https://www.rd.com/article/what-is-instagram/
Learn about Instagram and how it's used by people around the globe

Index